What Do I Do Now, LORD?

CHRIS JONES

Art by Judy Swanson

Augsburg Publishing House
Minneapolis, Minnesota

WHAT DO I DO NOW, LORD?

Copyright © 1976 Augsburg Publishing House

Library of Congress Catalog Card No. 76-3860

International Standard Book No. 0-8066-1539-7

Scripture quotations from the Revised Standard Version (RSV) of the Bible, copyright 1946, 1952, and 1971 by the Division of Christian Education of the National Council of Churches. Scripture quotations from the Living Bible (LB) copyright © 1971 by Tyndale House Publishers, are used by permission.

MANUFACTURED IN THE UNITED STATES OF AMERICA

CONTENTS

PREFACE

A boy's life is not all fun and games. You will have problems in your life. Everyone has problems—big problems, little problems, everyday problems.

Sometimes it helps to hear and read how others face problems and find answers for them.

In this book you will read stories based on real-life problems. You will read about answers, too—how boys like you solved their problems.

Problems can make us bitter.

Problems can make us better.

We can let problems win over us.

Or we can win over our problems—with God's help.

Some problems go away after a time. Many problems we have to tackle head-on. A few problems cannot be cured; they can only be endured.

For every problem God has promised help, either to overcome it or to live with it. At the end of each story you will find a quotation from God's Word. One thing we can do when we have problems is to hang onto God's promises.

Another thing we can do is to talk to God about our problems. At the end of each story you will also find a prayer to help you start talking to God about your problem. Then you can go on and talk with God in your own words.

God has promised that he will always hear you and answer you. And, best of all, he has promised to be with you.

In the Face of Fear

"As soon as everyone is back," Mr. Taylor announced, "we'll take a couple of hours off so you can go swimming."

The group cheered although they didn't really mind leaving camp to gather firewood. The trek into the north country was only three weeks away, and the Teen League from the Norton Community Church were anxious to prove to Mr. Taylor that they were fit and ready to go.

Only Alan Swanson received the news about swimming with an inward groan.

"You going swimming this afternoon?" Kevin Rialto asked Alan with a sneer.

Alan hesitated. Kevin had been needling him ever since the last camp. Alan figured he was still irritated from the swim meet last summer when Alan had soundly beaten Kevin in the 100 meters.

"Probably not," Alan replied, brushing past him.

Kevin grabbed his shoulder. "Why not?" he asked. "You were the only one who didn't swim yesterday, and you didn't swim at all at the other training camps. What's the matter?" the sneer became nastier. "Lost your nerve?"

Alan shook himself free. "Of course not. I can swim better than you can and you know it."

Kevin's face lit up. "Prove it!" he cried. "I'll race you across the river and back. Right now —up at Sandy Beach!" Kevin was practically jumping with anticipation.

Alan shook his head. "I'm not swimming," he said loudly. Then he pushed past the group of boys and strode towards his tent. As he went, he noticed Mr. Taylor watching him thought-fully, from the edge of the campsite. He had obviously heard everything.

Alan snatched up his fishing pole and tackle box. *That Kevin Rialto was going to spoil everything,* he thought angrily. *Now that Mr. Taylor knew he wouldn't go swimming, maybe he wouldn't let him go up to Thunder Bay.*

Alan waited until all the group had left for Sandy Beach, then he picked his way through the bushes to the river. He chose a sunny, shel-tered spot with a soft grassy bank and a tree to lean on.

Soon the warm sunshine and shouts of fun and laughter from the family campsite, across the river, eased his angry mood. *He had to admit it*, he thought, casting his line into the swiftly flowing river, *he had lost his nerve. But so would Kevin Rialto if he'd been the one to be caught under that sailboat last summer*, he thought defensively.

Alan shuddered. Just thinking about it made his skin crawl. It had happened at the end of the summer and was the worst experience of his whole life. He and dad had rented a small sailboat while they were up at Lake Superior. They had been sailing for about an hour when a squall blew up. Somehow they couldn't get back into the shelter of the bay. The water whipped into a frenzy, churning and boiling, and the waves grew higher and higher. Suddenly a large wave reared up and caught the boat sideways. At the same moment a vicious blast of wind took the sail, and the boat flipped over.

Luckily Alan was wearing his life jacket, but when he bobbed up out of the dark water he was trapped under the upturned boat. He was dazed and winded, and for a few terrible moments panic gripped him. He thrashed about trying to get out.

The memory flooded back to him as clearly as though it had happened yesterday. Thank

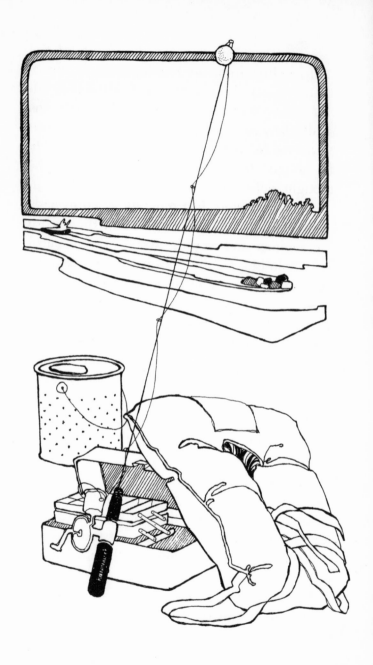

goodness dad had rescued him. Alan was sure he could never have saved himself.

But the worst wasn't over. For the next half hour they had clung desperately to the boat waiting to be rescued, expecting any moment to be swept away by the threatening waves. Since then, Alan had never swum again.

He pushed the unpleasant scene from his mind, reeled in his line and cast it again. Across the river several small children came down to the water's edge to play. A small rowboat had been hauled up onto the sandy shore and they were climbing in it, pretending they were at sea.

As the afternoon wore on Alan began to doze. The fish weren't biting, and the warm sunshine and fresh air made him sleepy.

He wasn't sure how long he'd been asleep, when urgent cries dragged him back to reality. He sat up and looked all around. His fishing line with its red float was still bobbing in the water, and the sun filtered through the tall pine trees shading much of the river. Now all he heard was the gurgle and splash of the river. He stood up. Had he dreamed it?

Then he heard the cries again. He scanned the river carefully. Downstream a movement caught his eye.

There, almost lost in the shade-dappled water, was the rowboat that had been beached across the river. A small boy was standing in it, and the craft was tipping dangerously.

"Mom! mom!" the child cried, his voice rising in panic.

Somehow the boy had pushed the boat off into the river, and now the current was moving him swiftly downstream. There was no sign of anyone on the other bank.

Alan pulled off his shirt and kicked off his shoes. Then he cupped his hands to his mouth.

"Sit down!" he yelled. "Sit down in the boat! I'm coming to get you."

Without another thought he splashed into the water. For a moment as the water washed over his head, a feeling of panic rose in his throat. The terror he'd felt then, as the waves swirled around him, returned, and threatened to swamp him. He surfaced, and the child's terrified cries swept away the nightmare memories.

In a few moments of strong swimming he reached the boat. The child was sitting down now, crying softly and clinging to the sides. Alan spoke to him in a calm voice, and gradually the crying stopped.

"Now you stay sitting there, and we'll be back on shore right away," Alan said. He grasped the stern of the boat and began to kick, pushing the boat ahead of him.

By the time he reached the other shore, out of breath and legs aching, several adults were waiting. The child began to cry again, as his mother scooped him into her arms. Alan flopped onto the bank, getting his breath back.

Then he heard someone call him from the other side of the river. The Teen Leaguers were back from their swimming. Alan jumped up, waded out into the river again, and swam over to them.

"We just got back when we heard the commotion," someone said. "That was quite a rescue."

Alan was embarrassed. "It was nothing," he said. "You'd have done the same if you'd been here."

Then Mr. Taylor stepped forward. "I'd say it was a pretty courageous thing to do, for someone who nearly drowned in a boating accident last year."

Alan looked at him in amazement. "You knew?" he said.

Mr. Taylor nodded. "Your father told me all about it, soon after it happened. I guessed why you wouldn't join us when we went swimming. But I wasn't worried. I knew a fine swimmer like you would come through when it really counted. You'll be a great asset to our camp next month."

At that moment Kevin Rialto sidled up. "Say," he muttered. "I'm sorry for bugging you this afternoon. Tell us what happened last year, when you nearly drowned."

"Yeah," the others begged, "tell us about it." And Alan found himself surrounded by admiring friends.

> I can do everything God asks me to with the help of Christ who gives me strength and power.

Phil. 4:13 LB

Dear God, some things in my life seem to need special help from you. Please give me your strength in overcoming them. Thank you for not leaving me to face the hard things alone.

Jumping to Conclusions

"Come on, William. Hurry up," Russ called back to his hiking partner. *Of all the sharp kids that were at the Yoho River Camp, why did he get stuck with William? William, who couldn't climb ropes, couldn't swim fifty yards, and couldn't even make the grade with an axe because he got too tired. If a person didn't have the stamina to compete, why come to a camp like this?* Russ wondered.

Their assignment was to hike eight miles to the lodge at the foot of Twin Falls, pick up a note proving they'd reached there, and return before dark by a different route.

But William had held them back, and it was almost two o'clock when they reached Twin Falls.

High across the other side of the valley a

sheer cliff towered, and over the edge, a pair of waterfalls tumbled side by side for a dizzying fifty feet or more. The sun behind the mountainside illuminated the spray with a back light that made it look like a thousand diamonds tossed into the air.

Russ forgot his irritation for a moment as he watched. Then for the first time he noticed the large black clouds that loomed up behind them. The sunshine disappeared and great drops of rain spattered on them. Quickly they ran to the shelter of the lodge. By the time they received their proof-note, it had stopped, but dark clouds threatened more showers, so they took their yellow plastic raincoats out of their backpacks.

Russ didn't want to wait any longer. They were already later than he had planned, and he figured the rain could make the trail difficult to find.

Badgering William to hurry, Russ set off down the new trail. The raincoats hampered them as they walked, and raindrops dripped off the bushes down their necks. To add to their misery, thick mud clung to their boots, making them heavy and unwieldy. Here and there the trail disappeared in a sea of mud. Rain-soaked leaves bowed low, hiding the way ahead.

Late in the afternoon the showers turned to a steady drizzle, but Russ was too busy watching for the trail to care. He was sure they were moving in the right direction but he hadn't seen the trail for 20 minutes.

"Do you think we've missed the trail?" William called from behind.

Russ stopped and William almost slid into him. "Let's take a look at the map," Russ said. He didn't like to admit it, but he was a little worried.

William pulled off his backpack and began to hunt through it. "It's not here," he said in a small voice. "I think I left it at the lodge."

"Thanks a lot!" Russ snorted. Just when they really needed it!

"We'll have to keep moving in this direction then," he said. "With this weather, it will be dark in an hour."

The thick undergrowth had ripped their raincoats in so many places that they no longer protected them from the rain. But they plodded on, getting wetter and colder. And still the trail eluded them.

Russ began to get alarmed. Getting lost in this kind of country could be serious. It was almost dark now, and fear gripped him. He looked around desperately, wondering which way to go. He began to move off again when he noticed William wasn't following.

"Come *on!*" Russ yelled at him, furious now. But William shook his head.

18

"It's almost dark and we're lost," he said, stating the obvious in a calm voice. "One of the first rules of survival when you're lost is to stay put. We should find ourselves some shelter and stay right here. That way anyone looking for us will have a chance to find us."

Russ knew he was right and he was irritated. "If it hadn't been for you, we wouldn't be in this mess now!" he said bitterly.

But William didn't answer. "Listen!" he said suddenly. Russ listened. He couldn't hear anything.

"It's the river!" William said excitedly. "Listen!"

Russ listened again. Sure enough, what he had taken to be the rain on the leaves was the sound of a rushing river.

"Come on" William exclaimed. "Let's get down to the river." And he dashed off, leaving Russ to follow.

What's so special about the river! Russ thought. Ahead of him, William forced a way through the bushes until he stood on a rocky bank, outlined against the foaming river.

Russ clambered after him, but as he reached the rocks, his muddy boots slipped and his legs shot out from under him. His arms flailed wildly, and the next second he landed hard on the rocks. A shooting pain ripped down his right leg and he lay there moaning.

"I think I've pulled a muscle," he said through clenched teeth, fighting waves of nausea as the pain tore at his leg.

"Here," William shouted in his ear above the roar of the water. "Lean on me. I see a small cave in the rocks over there. Think you can make it?" Very slowly the two boys moved through the gloom.

The cave wasn't very roomy, but an overhanging ledge kept it dry. Russ sank back against the wall. He must have stayed there several minutes before he became aware of William moving around.

"What are you doing?" he asked. William had emptied his backpack and then eased Russ's pack off his back.

"We can't be far from camp now," he said, "but you'll never make it. I'm going to make you as comfortable as possible." He folded the packs to make a cushion and tucked them behind Russ's back. "Now, I'll go and get help."

"Go and get help!" exclaimed Russ, suddenly angrier than ever. "How do you think you're going to find your way back to camp now? We couldn't even find the trail in the day light!" he exclaimed.

"It's not so difficult," William said simply. "I'll follow the river."

Russ's mouth dropped open. Follow the river! Why hadn't he thought of that?

But William was busy again. He had taken

off his ragged plastic raincoat and was tearing it into long strips. "I couldn't get any wetter," he explained, "so I'll tie these strips to the trees down by the river and they will serve as markers for the rescue party."

He moved out into the darkness and a few minutes later he came back grinning. "That should do it" he said. "You can almost see them in the darkness, and with the big flashlights the rescue parties have they couldn't miss them."

Russ's teeth were beginning to chatter. William glanced at him. "The sooner I get help the better," he muttered. "Now don't you move. I'll be back with help in no time."

The next minute he was gone. Lying there in the darkness, Russ had plenty of time to think. Who would have thought William could be any help in an emergency. He certainly used his head. He'd always been told that there was more to wilderness survival than physical fitness. Now he wished he hadn't been so impatient. He hoped William would be okay, out in the forest alone.

He began to drift in and out of sleep.

Much later he stirred uneasily. The pain in his leg felt like a red-hot needle. Everything seemed unreal. Lights flashed in front of his eyes, among the trees. The lights became brighter and closer. Dark figures moved towards him. At last help had come.

"Where's William?" Russ asked immediately.

"He's resting. He'll have to go into town for a check-up in the morning," a gruff voice answered. It was the camp director.

"Is he all right?" Russ asked anxiously. "I wouldn't have made it without him."

"He seemed okay," the director replied, "but we're not taking any chances. He had a serious illness a year ago. He was a fine woodsman before that. Never missed a camp. He begged us to let him come on this one, and we did, even though we knew he hadn't completely regained his strength."

Russ felt guilty. So *that's* why William couldn't do any of those things.

In no time at all he was wrapped in warm blankets and carried on a stretcher, back to camp.

William was waiting for him. "I couldn't rest until I was sure they'd found you," he explained.

"They came straight to the spot," Russ said from the stretcher. "I guess they couldn't miss your markers. Thanks," he added, "Thanks for everything. I'm sure glad it was you I went with on the hike."

William grinned. "We'll do it again," he said, "when your leg's better. Only this time we'll do it right."

"You bet!" Russ exclaimed, "and there isn't anyone I'd rather go with!"

> You have no right to criticize your brother or look down on him.
>
> Rom. 14:10 LB

Forgive me, Father, for misjudging others, for jumping to conclusions, for being too full of myself to see others clearly.

What Should I Be?

The library book fell open at a double-page photograph of a gray whale. Brian leaned back in his chair. The photo was magnificent! The enormous gray-barnacled nose of the whale thrust out of foaming water, and the camera had caught the giant tail in a massive flip.

He turned the pages of *The Ocean World*, looking at the photographs and reading the captions. The world of dolphins, sharks, and whales fascinated him. Brian wanted to learn everything he could about it. *Someday I'll be an oceanographer,* he decided.

After he had finished looking at the pictures, he settled back in the chair to read the text. But the print was small and there were many words in Latin—at least that's what Brian figured it was. Scientific books always seemed to contain a lot of Latin terms.

Before long, Brian began to lose interest in the book. Perhaps oceanography wasn't his field after all. He was irritated at himself. *Why couldn't he make up his mind?*

When his dad came home a little later, Brian met him with a question. "How old were you when you decided you were going to be a building contractor?" he asked, thinking of the beautiful homes dad built.

"That's hard to say, Brian," dad answered. "You see, I was an engineer to begin with, and then I decided to go into building. That was 13 years ago. I decided to take up engineering when I was in college, and then I became interested in design, so I began designing houses and building them. Sometimes one career leads into another, I guess."

Brian screwed up his nose. Dad's answer wasn't very satisfactory. "How will I ever decide what I want to be when I keep changing my mind?" he said. "Last year I was sure I was going to be a professional football player. This year I've thought about being an airplane pilot, a photographer, and now an oceanographer. How can I make up my mind?"

"Don't be in such a hurry, Brian," dad laughed. "You can try out all kinds of ideas while you're still a teen-ager. Why don't you study about different careers—find out more about them, see how your interests and abilities fit in with the career you're considering.

But take your time. You may have talents you haven't even discovered yet."

Brian shrugged. That didn't seem very likely. Besides, he didn't like not knowing what his plans were. He wanted to decide now. *I guess I'll be an oceanographer, anyway,* he thought. *I'll just have to study all those long words—and maybe learn Latin too.*

The next day at school, Brian told his friend Chuck what he had decided.

"Sounds good," Chuck said. "I haven't decided what I'm going to be yet. I may be a garage mechanic like my Uncle Ted."

"A garage mechanic!" chipped in Bob Downs who had joined them. "Not me! I don't want to be around that smelly gas and oil all day. I'm going to join the Marines. It's good pay, and you get to travel a lot."

By now several other boys had joined the group and they all had comments to add.

"I'm not joining the Marines," said one. "No one's going to boss me around. I'm going to have my own business like my dad."

"I'm going to be a bag boy at the supermarket," said another grinning. "That way I won't have to worry about grades or college or anything."

"Sure," added a third, "but you'll never have much money. I'm going to get a job that makes a lot of money, like a doctor or lawyer or something."

"Yeah, but look at all the hours you have to work as a doctor," Brian pointed out. "What's the good of all that money if you don't have time to enjoy it?"

The discussion continued back and forth until the bell rang. Everyone had his own idea of what was the best kind of job.

Sure is a complicated thing, this business of deciding what you want to be, Brian thought. It seemed as soon as he made up his mind, something else occurred to him. What was it dad had said? "Take your time. You may have talents you haven't even discovered yet." What kind of talents could he have that he didn't already know about?

Several days later Brian's home room teacher asked him to stay after school for a few minutes. "We're looking for five or six eighth-graders who would be willing to help children as tutors in the elementary schools," Mr. Burnley said. "We are choosing students carefully, because this is a new program and we want to be sure it will work. The rest of the staff think that you would be a good choice, Brian. It's a wonderful opportunity if you are at all interested in a teaching career," he continued. "What do you think? Would you like to try?"

Brian didn't hesitate. He hadn't considered a teaching career, but the idea of tutoring appealed to him. He liked young kids, and if the other teachers thought he could do it, he was willing to try.

At first it felt strange going into the second and third grade classrooms under the watchful eye of their teacher, but soon he became so interested in what he was doing that he forgot about being shy. He moved about the classroom, from student to student, helping them with their problems.

One day the classroom teacher asked Brian to take Matthew Raynes aside and help him with his addition. Matthew was small for his age. His blond hair kept falling over his eyes, and he kept brushing it aside.

Looking over Matthew's math paper, Brian soon spotted his problem. Not only was he forgetting to carry the tens, but his figures were so jumbled Brian couldn't tell in which column the figures should be.

First Brian showed Matthew how to write his figures in neat columns. Then Brian explained about the carrying figures. At first Matthew didn't understand at all, and he brushed at his hair. But Brian began again and patiently explained the process. At each step he gave Matthew the chance to tell what to do next. At last, by the end of the lesson, Brian felt Matthew understood more clearly.

But the next day when Brian returned to the classroom, he found Matthew had forgotten everything. At least he had copied the figures in neat columns, and Brian praised him for that. Then he set to work explaining the process once more. Again Matthew kept pushing his hair, but by the end of the lesson Brian felt the young second-grader had begun to relax a little. He even thought Matthew had finally grasped the process of carrying tens. But would he forget it, Brian wondered. There were no more tutoring classes until next Tuesday, so he would have to wait and see.

On Monday afternoon, after school, Brian was cycling down to the football field when someone called after him. He slammed on his brakes and skidded to a halt.

It was Matthew, brushing his hair to one side as usual, but grinning broadly. "Guess what happened to me today," he said.

Brian shrugged good naturedly. "What happened?" he said.

"I got every one of my math problems right," Matthew replied, looking like he'd just found a five-dollar bill.

Brian stared in amazement. "Fantastic!" he shouted.

"Thanks to you!" Matthew added.

"Thanks to your hard work, you mean," Brian said, giving Matthew a friendly punch in the shoulder. "Keep up the good work," he said. He began to move off.

"See you tomorrow," Matthew called as Brian cycled away.

A feeling of satisfaction swept over Brian. It sure felt good to know how much he had helped Matthew. Perhaps he would make a good teacher. Maybe he did have some hidden talents, as dad suggested. Well, no sense in deciding right away. Maybe he'd have the chance to try out other ideas as he had with teaching. That seemed like a good way to help a person make up his mind.

But for now, teaching would be his goal—until he discovered something he liked better.

> I will instruct you (says the Lord) and guide you along the best pathway for your life.
>
> Ps. 32:8 lb

O Lord, I think I could do many things, and yet I know I will only be truly happy doing your will. Thank you for promising to guide me, and help me to be willing to follow.

I Want to Be My Own Boss

The sun streamed in the window of Ben's bedroom at his family's clifftop cabin. *Just the day to go to Barren Rock*, Ben thought.

Ben and his dad had come out to the cabin for a few days to spend some time together. As a doctor, dad didn't have a lot of spare time, but two or three times a year they would leave mom and Alice and Kathy behind, and the two of them would come out here to Crescent Bay. Then they would do some fishing or explore around in the rock pools.

Ben looked forward to this time most of all. Here at Crescent Bay he didn't have his two older sisters constantly picking at him, telling him what to do and how to behave. All that bossing made Ben long for the day when he could be his own boss. That's why it was so great to get away with dad like this. Dad never bossed him around like the girls did. Dad let him make his own decisions.

"Well, Ben, what are we going to do today?" dad asked as they cleared the dishes after breakfast.

"How about going over to Barren Rock when the tide goes out?" Ben suggested. Barren Rock was a small island about half a mile off the beach at Crescent Bay. Last year the brown pelican was nesting there, and Ben loved to watch the antics of the big bird. It flew with large wing flaps, and then if it spied a fish it dropped like a stone and disappeared under water. Moments later it would emerge with a silver fish wriggling in its large beak. Barren Rock would be a great place to go today. When the tide was out like today, the rock could be reached by walking over the sand.

Dad hesitated. "I'd better check on the tides first."

"The tide's going out, dad," Ben interrupted.

"I know it is, son."

"Well then, what's to stop us?" said Ben. The more he thought about the idea, the more anxious he was to go. Through the living room window the ocean gleamed like silver, and the rock loomed dark and inviting against the sunshine.

"At this time of the year . . ." dad began,

but the telephone interrupted him, and he went to answer it.

Ben finished putting the dishes away and went over to the window. Barren Rock looked magnificent. The tide was already half way out of the bay, leaving flat rocks full of small pools, and then a stretch of sandy beach, its wet surface shimmering in the sunshine.

Dad's face was serious as he hung up the phone. "I'm sorry, Ben, an emergency has come up and I'll have to drive back to town immediately. It'll take a couple of hours, but I'll be back after lunch. Do you want to come with me and spend the day in town?"

Ben made a face. "Do I have to, dad?"

"No," his father said, moving into the bedroom, gathering his things to leave. "No, I think you could stay here by yourself for a few hours." Ben's heart leaped. Just what he would enjoy. He would be his own boss for a few hours.

"Okay, dad," he said.

"But don't go over to Barren Rock today. Wait until I get back. We can go tomorrow if the tide's right."

"But dad . . ." Ben began. But his father was out of earshot. Ben was disappointed. He glanced back at the rock. *I guess it'll wait until tomorrow,* he thought, *but I sure wish I could go now.*

"Remember, I'm leaving you in charge, Ben,"

said dad reappearing with his jacket and brief-case. "Use the phone if there are any emergen-cies. Have a good time and I'll see you about three this afternoon." The next minute his fa-ther was gone.

Ben made himself some peanut butter and honey sandwiches, put an apple and a few cookies in a bag, and set off for the beach.

The sun was warm and the tide pools full of interesting creatures. Ben poked around in the pools looking for hermit crabs. He liked to see them stick their claws out of the sea shell they had adopted for their home. Next he tried feed-ing tiny shrimp to the flower-like sea anemo-nes. In a large pool he found some long, thin, silver fish and tried to catch them with his hands, but they were too quick for him.

At last Ben began to feel hungry. He clam-bered back over the slippery rocks to the large flat dry rock on which he had left his lunch. He began to pull out a sandwich when he glanced up at the ocean. He noticed something strange. The tide was farther out than Ben had ever seen before. The white line of surf churned far beyond Barren Rock. Ben was amazed. The rock looked so near it seemed it would take only a matter of minutes to reach it. But he remembered his promise to his fa-ther.

Ben gazed out at the ocean. *The tide was so far out it would be hours before it came in again,* he reasoned. *It was perfectly safe to go. After all he was his own boss, wasn't he?* Making up his mind in a flash, Ben put his lunch together again and set off for Barren Rock.

As he walked across the soft wet sand, in his imagination he could hear his sister Alice's voice taunting him, "Children, obey your parents in the Lord." Alice was always quoting the Bible at him. *Not that there was anything wrong with the Bible, but what made Alice think she was so perfect and he was always wrong? Anyway, dad would understand, wouldn't he?* A small doubt was there, but Ben ignored it.

It was a perfect afternoon for the rock. Sitting up high and eating his lunch, Ben felt as if he owned the island. After he'd eaten, he explored.

He found the pelicans' favorite spot, and taking care not to go too close, he watched. They sat in rows, nodding their heads at one another. Some were sleeping with their long necks doubled. Once in a while, one would stretch himself and take off in a glide so easy that Ben wondered how he managed to keep airborne.

Completely absorbed in watching the birds, Ben forgot all about the tide. Suddenly he remembered. He looked up and, with a stab of fear, saw that it had already crept up behind the island and was putting out a long tongue across the sand between the rock and the beach.

He scrambled swiftly down the side of the rock. The tide was moving fast, he noticed nervously. He began to run across the wet sand, but it was getting softer as the tide came in, and his feet sank.

At last, out of breath and a little frightened, Ben reached the long tongue of water. It was much wider now and had already joined the water coming around from the other side of the island. It was swirling and surging, and Ben realized that it was almost to wide for him to swim across.

In a flash he knew he should have stayed on the rock. He whirled around, thinking to run back, but he was too late. The tide was already washing around the foot of the rock. Who would have believed the tide could come in so fast! He was completely cut off now, marooned on a sand bar.

He turned back to the beach and scanned it for some sign of life, but there was no one. He looked at the water again. He'd have to try and swim for it. It was his only chance.

If only he'd listened to dad, he thought as he splashed into the water. He began to swim, but the surge of the current pulled against him. He was already tired from running across the sand. He swam a few strokes and then drifted, swam a few more and drifted again. He wasn't making any headway at all. The tide was pulling him sideways.

He turned on his back and floated for a while, resting his aching legs. After a few moments he tried swimming again. As he raised his head to breathe, a ray of hope swept through him. The drift of the tide had pulled him sideways towards the mouth of the bay. If he could just make those rocks at the point, he would be safe. But if he missed them, the current would sweep him out to sea.

With renewed strength Ben pulled across the sideways drift of the current. Then he rested and let himself drift again. Little by little, swimming and drifting, he moved in zig-zag fashion closer to the rocks until at last they were within reach.

Quickly he scrambled up the seaweed-covered rocks. He couldn't stop now, although his legs and shoulders ached with exertion. In a short time these rocks would be covered too. He'd have to climb the cliff to keep out of the reach of the tide. He looked up. Normally it wouldn't have been too difficult. It wasn't very high, but now every step was an effort and every muscle strained. He clutched at the rocks with his fingers and stubbed his toes as he climbed, until at last he reached the top.

There he collapsed on the wiry grass and took in huge gulps of air. It wasn't until he had rested his aching arms and legs and could breathe normally again that he became aware of his cut fingers and toes and scratched knees. Painfully, he stood up and limped back to the cabin.

It was while he was looking for the first-aid kit that he saw the newspaper lying on the kitchen table where dad had left it. A heavy black title caught his eye:

SPRING TIDES DUE THIS WEEK

Unusually high and low tides are due at Crescent Bay this week. Visitors to our area should be especially aware of these dangerous tides. Occurring four times in the year, the tide ebbs to an extremely low point and then returns to the flood tide mark with unusual speed. The name "Spring Tide" has been applied to this phenomenon because the water returns from its ebb with such speed and strength that it would appear to be bubbling up from hidden underground springs.

So that's why dad wouldn't let him go to Barren Rock! The Spring Tides. Ben had heard of them, but didn't know what they were. He wandered over the living room window. The waves were pounding the cliffs at the point of the bay where Ben had finally reached the shore. He watched the spray burst against the cliff and shuddered. It had been a close call.

And he'd thought he was smart enough to make his own decisions.

There's nothing wrong with wanting to be your own boss, even dad said that. Just so long as you don't decide you know everything, Ben thought. Some things come by experience, he decided—and that was *one* experience he wouldn't forget.

> It is good for a young man to be under discipline.
>
> Lam. 3:27 LB

Sometimes I wish I could grow up all at once. It's hard to understand that there are many things I can't do yet just because I'm not old enough. Lord, give me patience and willingness to learn.

Bothered by a Bully

"Crash!" Neil's bike collided with Stan's and the clatter could be heard all the way down at Judy Runkle's house. She came to the sidewalk and stared up the street; then she began to laugh.

After he had recovered from the impact, Neil had to admit that Stan did look pretty funny tangled up in his bike with his cap down over his eyes. Neil had swerved at the last minute and didn't even come off his bike. But Stan hadn't seen him until they'd hit, and being bigger than Neil, he had come down hard.

"Oh, wow! Stan," Judy giggled, her voice carrying up the hill. "You caught it that time! You look so funny!" and she laughed loudly.

Stan pushed the cap back out of his eyes. "Why don't you look where you're going!" he yelled at Neil. He looked angry and embarrassed.

Neil protested. "Me! Why don't you look where *you're* going!"

Stan disentangled his large frame from the bicycle. "If anything's broken, you'll have to pay for it," he bellowed, getting redder and redder as Judy's laughter still drifted up the street.

Then he seized the curved handle of the gear shift and it flipped loosely. "See what you've done? Now the gears are broken and this isn't my bike."

Neil recognized the bike. It belonged to Stan's older brother, Barry. "Those gears were broken months ago!" Neil protested hotly, "Barry told me."

"Oh no they weren't," Stan said. "Just wait until I tell him."

Neil ignored him. He knew the gears were broken before. Stan was just embarrassed and looking for something to blame on him. Neil mounted his bike again and rode away with Stan's threats echoing after him.

It was too bad, he figured, as he pedaled faster. He'd managed to upset the biggest bully in the junior high school. As well as being a full year older, Stan was several sizes larger than Neil and someone he tried to stay away from. Stan was always threatening, pushing, or hitting someone. He wouldn't be likely to forget today's embarrassment in a hurry.

Just as Neil expected, the next night Stan and his friends waited for him as he got off the school bus. Neil straightened the books under his arm, his heart thumping.

"Hi, Neil," said Stan, a leer on his face. "When are you going to pay me for busting my brother's gears?"

"Yeah, Neil," said Dusty Carter stepping in front of him and bumping him with his shoulder. "Oops! Sorry. Did I bump into you? Sorry about that."

Roger Porter circled behind him and Neil glanced over his shoulder. Too late! Roger came at him arms outstretched and palms flat in a well aimed shove. Neil slammed up against Stan.

"Hey! Watch where you're going!" Stan yelled, grabbing Neil by the back of the collar. Then he clenched his fist under Neil's nose and shook him threateningly. "Now you pay up for those gears, or you'll get what's coming to you."

"That's right," Dusty Carter added, advancing towards Neil again. "Otherwise—see these books?" he said, pointing to the books Neil was still clutching. "If you don't. . . ." With a a swift punch he knocked the books out of Neil's arms. They shot up in the air, papers and pages flying.

Then Stan pushed Neil into the bushes, and the three bullies ran away laughing loudly.

Neil picked himself up. He was all right except for a few scratches. If he ever caught up with Stan Benton on his own—but in his heart Neil knew he was no match for Stan. Broad-chested and stocky, Stan could make mincemeat out of Neil's slim and wiry frame.

He snatched up the rest of his papers and ran home. Safely in the house he ran up to his room and threw his books and papers in a jumble on the bed. *That Stan Benton!* he thought angrily, *Now he'll make life miserable for me until I pay up. I've got to think of something to stop him.*

Neil sat on the edge of his bed thinking hard.

I'll never win by trying to fight him. Even if I got all my friends to help, Stan would just try to get back at me again some other time. It could go on forever. No, there must be a better way.

He kicked off his shoes, swung his legs around onto the bed and stretched out, staring at the ceiling.

I didn't break those gears, he thought. *I know I didn't. I wonder if Barry knows Stan's trying to get me to pay for them. I wonder if Barry even knows Stan was riding his bike yesterday. Stan was always riding Barry's bike. Didn't he have one of his own?* Then a thought occurred to him. Suppose he offered to let Stan ride *his* bicycle one afternoon. It was almost new and had ten speeds. Stan would like that and then maybe he'd leave Neil alone.

Yeah, he argued with himself, *but who wanted to do anything nice for Stan after today! Besides Stan would think he was doing it because he was scared.*

He continued turning all these things over in his mind. If he could only get Barry to admit in front of Stan that the gears had been broken long ago. That wouldn't make Stan any friendlier, but it would prove a point.

At last, little by little a plan began to form. A plan that would put Stan in his place. It would show him that Neil wasn't going to be bullied by him, but it would be an offer of friendship too.

The next day was Saturday and Neil knew that if he went over right after breakfast, Stan and Barry would both be home. As he parked his bike against the fence, Neil noticed Barry's bike with the broken gears parked close by.

Neil's heart was pounding, but he was determined to go through with his plan. He rang the front door bell. Stan answered the door. He looked surprised to see Neil.

"May I speak to Barry, please?" Neil said quickly, taking advantage of Stan's surprise.

"Barry!" Stan called over his shoulder, responding automatically. Then he growled suspiciously, "What do you want to talk to Barry

45

for?" But Barry came to the door before Neil could reply.

Neil led Barry out to the driveway, telling him he wanted to show him something. Stan followed, looking even more suspicious.

"How long have the gears been broken on your bike?" Neil asked Barry, walking over to it.

"Wait a minute," Stan interrupted, looking uncomfortable, "you broke. . . ."

Neil stepped in front of Stan. Inwardly he was quaking, but he spoke firmly. "I came to talk to Barry."

"Yeah," said Barry, looking annoyed at his brother's interruption.

Stan stopped abruptly. He looked puzzled.

Barry began to flick the loose gear shift back and forth. "This has been broken since last summer," he said. "Why?"

"Well, Stan seems to think I broke it last week when he raced out of the driveway and we collided," Neil answered.

"I didn't say that," Stan protested, "I mean I . . . ." his voice faded.

"Are you throwing your weight around again?" Barry said, turning to Stan. "You know that gear shift has been broken for months. What are you trying to pull?" Barry grew angrier as he spoke. "And how come you went chasing out into the street on my bike without looking? You're lucky it was only Neil you

46

crashed into. Keep your hands off my bike from now on. The way you ride, it will be no good to anyone. Don't ride it again. Do you hear?"

Stan wilted under his brother's words. Neil almost felt sorry for him. He didn't look like such a bully now.

Barry continued, turning to Neil, "Don't take any notice of him, kid. You didn't break those gears," and he strode back into the house.

Stan was silent for a moment. Then he scowled "Thanks a lot!" he said glumly. "There goes my transportation."

"Don't worry about that," Neil said, and he paused. He had to force himself to continue, but he had to do it if he really wanted to make his plan work. He took a deep breath, "You can borrow my bike," he finished. There! It was out.

Stan looked at him in amazement. "You're kidding!"

"No, I'm not. I mean it." Neil replied, feeling better about it now that he'd said it.

"You mean, after what I did to you, you'd let me borrow your bike?"

"If you promise to take care of it."

Stan's face lit up and he walked over to Neil's ten-speed. He ran his hands over the handle bars and patted the seat.

"Hey, I misjudged you," he said softly. "You're okay. Look—I'm sorry for the way. . . ."

"Forget it," Neil replied.

"I'll be careful," Stan said. "I never had a bike as nice as this one," he added wistfully.

Neil watched Stan's face as he tried the bike out for size. Maybe, if I got to know Stan better, he thought, I might even learn to like him.

> Love your enemies. Do good
> to those who hate you.
>
> Luke 6:27 LB

Father, when others are mean to me, give me the courage to stand up for what I know is right. Help me to love even those who would make my life miserable. Help me to love the way you love us.

Going into the Hospital

"Okay!" Gene Henson bellowed above the clatter. "Everyone sit on the floor and we'll wind it up until next week."

Phil heaved his chair up on one of the stacks lined up against the wall and joined the group arranging themselves comfortably on the floor. *Wonder what they'll do next week*, Phil thought. *Wish I weren't going to miss it.* He started to feel worried, but Gene began to speak.

A senior at Eisenhower High School, Gene, with his tall frame, thick black hair, and dark-rimmed glasses looked like a brain. But in spite of his serious face, Gene was the greatest guy Phil had ever known. Behind those glasses and that thick black hair was a sense of humor and spirit of fun that made Gene Henson the most popular leader the youth group had ever had. As if that weren't enough, Gene was also captain of the Eisenhower basketball team, and basketball was the only thing closer to Phil's heart than the Adventurers.

"Next week," Gene began, "we have a special project. We'll be going down to Mrs. Langshaw's place to help clean up her yard."

The group groaned.

"I *knew* you'd all enjoy doing that," Gene grinned, "that's why I volunteered your help." His grin grew broader as the groans grew louder.

"Okay, okay. I get the message," he said. "But here's the good part. If we go and clean up Mrs. Langshaw's yard, she's promised to donate $50."

"Wow! Fifty dollars—now that's more like it," someone said.

"We're going to need some equipment," Gene went on, "Phil, your dad's got one of those lawn sweepers, hasn't he—the kind that sweeps up the leaves? Think you could bring it?"

Phil hesitated, "I—I'm not going to be here," he said, "but I'm sure dad will let you borrow it."

"You going away?" Gene asked.

"Not exactly," Phil paused. He wasn't going to say anything more, but everyone was waiting for an explanation. "I—well, I'm going into the hospital next week." He could feel himself flushing with embarrassment. He didn't mean to keep it a secret, but he didn't want everyone making a fuss about it.

"Nothing serious, I hope," Gene said.

"No, just my tonsils," Phil replied, feeling slightly foolish. It sounded like something that should happen to a little kid, not a student in junior high school.

Nobody really paid much attention to his news, and the group continued to make plans for next week. Phil was glad when the time came for them to go home. He slipped out ahead of the others so that he wouldn't have to answer any questions.

Most of the time Phil tried not to think about going into the hospital. It was just a bit scary. He had never been in the hospital before and he wasn't sure what to expect. The trouble was, he decided, he was too old to admit that he was scared and too young to feel like an adult about it. If there was only some way he could avoid it.

He had racked his brains trying to come up with something. He had tried all the tactics he knew on his mother, but she wouldn't be persuaded. Now the operation was less than a week away.

As soon as he arrived home, Phil made straight for his room to get his basketball.

Shooting a few baskets was a good way to forget his problems.

"There's a letter for you, Phil," mom called from the kitchen. "It's on the dining room table."

A letter! Phil's heart bumped. There was only one letter he was waiting for and that was from the Julian Park Basketball Camp saying that he was eligible for the tryouts. It was the best camp in the state, and it was an honor just to be considered, let alone accepted, for the camp.

Phil detoured back to the dining room. There it was—a long white envelope with black embossed printing in the corner: Julian Park Basketball Camp.

Mother came into the dining room. Phil knew she was as excited as he. Mom and dad both backed him 100% in his basketball playing. They never missed a game.

His fingers fumbled as he opened the slim envelope.

Quickly he scanned the contents. "I made it!" he cried, "I made it! I made the tryouts!"

"Look!" he said and he handed the letter to his mother.

"Congratulations!" mother said with a big smile and she read the letter. Then her smile disappeared.

"Oh, Phil," she said. "Look at the dates of the tryouts. They're next Thursday evening." She handed the letter to him.

"Next Thursday! But that's when I am supposed to have the surgery," he cried. Then he paused. Something just occurred to him. Here was his opportunity. Mom and dad wouldn't make him miss the tryouts. They were as anxious for him to make the camp as he was to go.

"Well, that settles it," he began. "We'll just have to cancel the surgery. I don't really need it and. . . ."

But mom was shaking her head. "I'm sorry, Phil," she said. "You *must* have the surgery. Dr. Braden said there was no question about it. The hospitals are so full, we can't reschedule now. We've had to wait two months for this time slot."

Phil shook his head in disbelief. "You mean I can't make the tryouts?" he said, his voice rising. "I *have* to, mother! I have to!"

"Of course you do, Phil. But I'm sure we can reschedule your tryouts. There are sure to be several sessions, because they have so many applications. I'll call them in the morning before you go in for your doctor's appointment."

Phil relaxed a little. Maybe he wouldn't miss the tryouts altogether—but that still left him with the surgery to face. There must be something he could do to get out of it. Perhaps he could persuade Dr. Braden in a last-ditch effort tomorrow morning.

The next morning mom phoned the camp, as

she promised, and his tryout was set for next month instead.

On his way to Dr. Braden's office for his presurgery check-up, Phil planned a last-minute plea to Dr. Braden—a last-minute, all-out effort to avoid the surgery.

He began to rehearse a carefully worded statement.

"Hi there!" someone said heartily, as he entered the office.

Phil jerked back to reality. It was Gene Henson. "What are you doing here?" Phil said in surprise.

"Looks like I'll be in for another operation on my knee pretty soon," Gene said, pulling a wry face.

"Your knee?" Phil said.

"Yeah," Gene answered. "The one I injured in a basketball game two years ago. Been in and out of the hospital four or five times since then, trying to get it fixed. I'm afraid it'll never be the same though," he said. "Looks like this will be my last season of basketball."

"Oh no!" said Phil in concern. "You're so good everyone thought you'd make the pros."

"Yeah, well my game's been slipping this season, so I decided to face the facts. It's no use kidding yourself. It was hard to take at first, but I've got other things I enjoy doing too."

Gene breathed deeply, and then changed the

subject. "So how's your game going?" That was all Phil needed to launch into a discussion of the Julian Park tryouts.

After Gene's turn was called, Phil began to think. Gene had to have several operations—of his own choice too. And now, it was all for nothing. He'd never be as good at basketball again. It all made Phil's tonsil operation look pretty insignificant.

When it was Phil's turn, Dr. Braden checked him out thoroughly. "Well, you're in fine shape, except for your throat," he said. "All set for Thursday?" Phil nodded bleakly. After talking to Gene he couldn't bring himself to make the carefully worded plea he had planned. Instead, he dressed quickly and left the office as soon as possible.

When he got home Phil went out to shoot some baskets again. But he couldn't forget his conversation with Gene. A tonsil operation was nothing compared to what Gene had gone through. At least Phil's operation would be over and done with, and it wouldn't affect his game, except for a short time. He had an uncomfortable guilty feeling. He wished he hadn't tried to get out of it.

Phil shot one more basket and then went back into the house. He put his ball away and strode purposefully out to the kitchen.

"Mom," he said, "I'm just going up to the library to get some books on basketball."

Mom nodded, "Okay." she said.

Phil explained, "I figure I'm going to need something to read next week while I'm in the hospital."

> God is our refuge and strength, a very present help in trouble.
>
> Ps. 46:1

Thank you for your promise to be with me all the time. Please be with me when I have to do things I'm afraid of. Give me the courage to face the hard things in my life.

Out of Touch

Brad came running to the dock side, where his father was standing, his heart pounding with excitement. "Hey dad!" he yelled, "Jim Grimes said he'll take us out fishing tomorrow if we want to go with him. Can we go?"

Brad held his breath, waiting for his dad's answer. He *had* to say yes. In all the time they had come on vacation to Rockford Beach, Jim Grimes had never offered to take them fishing before. Jim was quite a few years older than Brad, and Brad envied his easy-going life. With his own fishing boat he had the freedom of the ocean. When his father died of a heart attack, Jim inherited an old fishing boat and immediately dropped out of school.

Dad hesitated. "Tomorrow's Sunday, Brad. We'll be going to church."

"Oh *dad!*" said Brad, his hopes dashed. "Do we *have* to go to church when we're on vacation?" He scowled and then he added, "Besides, I'm getting too big for church and Sunday school. Jim never goes."

"We're Christians in our family," dad said gently, "and we all go to church on Sundays. We're never too old to go to church."

"But I don't get anything out of it, dad."

"How much do you put into it, Brad?"

Brad dropped his head. He didn't put much into it, he knew. He fooled around in class when he could get away with it, and tuned out the pastor's sermon, Sunday by Sunday. It seemed such a waste of time to spend a couple of hours each week in church when there were so many other exciting things to do.

"Ask Jim if he can take us on Monday," said dad. "I'll be glad to go then."

Fortunately Jim agreed, and Brad was happy again.

Somehow Brad got through Sunday. He was sorry he had to spend two hours of such a beautiful day in a stuffy church, but when Monday dawned as beautiful as Sunday he was satisfied.

Dad loaded their fishing gear into the *Daisy Mae.* "Good of you to take us out, Jim," dad said to the teen-ager.

Jim nodded. "Glad for the company," he replied.

"Does the *Daisy Mae* have a very powerful engine?" dad asked.

"She's good enough on days like this when the water's not too rough," Jim replied casually. "Of course, the harbor mouth's a bit tricky to get in and out of, no matter what the weather. Strong current and freak waves—ever since they built that jetty half a mile north of here. She takes a bit o' handling to get her in and out safely."

"How about radar?" Brad asked.

"Haven't bothered with it." Jim said briefly. "Too expensive. Besides, when the weather's bad, I don't go out. I can come and go as I like."

"That's certainly a nice life," dad commented, "but don't you get bored?"

"Naw," said Bob. "I'm a natural-born drifter. No place to go to in a hurry. No pressure. Let the rest of the world break its neck. I'm not going to."

Brad looked at his dad to see what effect Jim's words were having on him. But dad's expression didn't betray his feelings. Jim's way of life did seem attractive, but somehow Brad felt felt there had to be more to life than just drifting in and out with the tide. Brad figured he would enjoy it for a while, but not forever.

Soon they began to chug their way out of the harbor. Now that the weekend was past there weren't many boats around. The water inside the harbor was like glass and the *Daisy Mae* cut through it with ease. Even the stretch through the harbor mouth was uneventful, although Brad could see heavy swells rising and falling, and the jagged black rocks at the base of the jetties looked ominous. Brad knew that Rockford Beach harbor had a reputation for being treacherous. He remembered last summer when they were on vacation here, even the harbor patrol boat capsized and was smashed to pieces.

Once they were far enough out to sea, Jim cut the engines and let the boat drift. Then they baited their hooks and threw out their lines.

For more than an hour they sat bobbing silently on the water. Dad caught a couple of small fish but had to throw them back. Jim sat the whole time with his back propped up against the cabin, pole in hand and a fishing hat pulled down over his eyes. For all Brad knew, he could be sleeping.

Brad felt sleepy too. The ocean shone like polished steel, and the gentle rocking of the boat added to his sleepy feeling. He stood up and moved his tackle to the other side of the boat, towards the horizon. There he would feel more of the gentle breeze. Far out to sea, the horizon was lost in a yellowish-gray haze, and the usually deep blue sky had a thin wash of mist over it. Brad hoped it didn't mean a change in the weather.

He leaned over the side of the boat. A jelly fish floated lazily by, and just out from the bow a fish jumped. He reeled in his line. Those bait-stealing fish! They seemed to know just how to nibble the bait off the hook without getting caught. He baited the hook again and cast out his line. Then he sat back against the cabin and waited.

Brad wasn't sure how long he sat there. Suddenly he realized he was feeling cold. He stood up and looked out to sea. The horizon was no longer there. The gray haze had become a bank of mist and rolled across the water.

Just then Jim tried to start the engine. Brad joined his dad on what should have been the landward side of the boat, but the shoreline had disappeared.

Brad moved into the cabin where Jim was coaxing the engine to life. At last it caught, and the boat began to move. Jim swung the bow in the direction of the coast. "Wind shifted," he muttered. "I must have fallen asleep."

"Fog's pretty thick," dad said, stepping into the cabin.

"I know, I know." said Jim looking worried. "Should have kept my eye on that fog bank. Been out there for days, just waiting for a change in the weather."

Dad looked worried too, but he didn't say anything. They chugged along for a while trying to peer through the damp fog. Brad looked at his dad, hoping for some encouraging sign. But dad had his head bowed. *Was he praying?* Brad wondered.

Eventually Jim changed direction slightly. "Can't be too far off shore now," he said. He cut the engine completely. The silence was almost deafening after the roar of the engine.

"What did you stop for?" Brad asked.

"Shh! I'm listening," Jim said.

Brad listened too, but all he could hear was the gentle lapping of the water and an occasional splash as a fish jumped. The mournful wail of a seagull sounded overhead. Suddenly Brad heard another sound—a gentle hum at first, but growing louder. Then Brad jumped as a deep horn blasted out of nowhere, echoing over the water. The hum became a roar.

Jim leapt into action. Brad had never seen him move so fast. He jabbed a button on the far side of the cabin and another blast of a horn filled the damp air. Suddenly a ship loomed out of the mist. The next moment it swerved as it saw the *Daisy Mae*. The bow of a pleasure launch sliced through the water only a few feet away.

"Phew! That was close," Jim said. Dad didn't speak, and Brad's legs had turned to jelly.

"Here, Brad," Jim said, "You man this horn. See that clock there with the second hand on it—every two minutes push that button, just like I did. Every two minutes now. Have you got that?"

Brad nodded. He felt jittery.

Jim started the engines, and the boat began to move. Then he asked dad to go up into the bow to be a lookout for them. "I'll move us in slowly. That boat's gone, but others will be caught in this. You listen for their horns and direct me from up front," Jim said. Then he muttered, "Sure wish I had a radio. Could use some communication right now."

They moved cautiously through the fog like a phantom ship. Then after about ten minutes Jim cut the engines again. He put his head outside the cabin and listened.

"Hear that?" he called to dad. "Two high-pitched wails a minute apart. That's the harbor fog horn." Then he turned to Brad. "Keep manning that horn," he said, "We're not through the worst of this yet. It'll be no joke finding the harbor mouth in this fog." The boat began to move again.

Brad wondered how on earth would they manage in the channel? The memory of those jagged black rocks came flooding back.

Just then dad waved his arms and Jim slowed the boat to a crawl. He stuck his head out of the cabin. "What is it?" he called.

"A boat ahead—portside," dad shouted.

They floated gently ahead and then out of the mist, the gray hull of the harbor patrol appeared. A patrolman stood at the bow, a megaphone at his mouth.

"Need help, buddy?" he called.

"Sure do!" Jim yelled back.

"Follow us," called the patrolman and the motorboat swung around and headed for the harbor entrance.

Dad came back into the cabin. "Praise the Lord for someone to follow," he said, his serious face white with strain. "Someone who knows the way ahead."

"You can say that again!" Jim said with feeling, his eyes steadily on the green and red lights of the patrol boat.

Safely home at last, Brad sipped on a mug of hot chocolate and gazed into the burning logs in the fireplace. It had been a scary experience out there alone, with no communication. Even dad had been worried. He'd prayed a lot, he said, while standing up there in the bow.

Maybe that's what going to church was all about—communication. How could you expect God to suddenly answer your prayers in an emergency, if you never talked to him before? He'd be in church next week for sure, Brad decided, and without complaints.

Seek the Lord and his strength, seek his presence continually.

1 Chron. 16:11 RSV

Being out of touch with you, O Lord, is like being lost in the fog. Forgive me for thinking I can take care of myself. Please guide me so my life will turn out right.

Why Don't I Have Any Friends?

It would have been a good game if José had known the rules, but he kept kicking the football instead of picking it up and running with it. Mike watched him in frustration. José charged at the ball and punted it with a flying kick right into the Fenwick's back yard. Dean ran to get it.

When José moved into his block, Mike had hoped they could become friends. But this game was ridiculous.

"I'm going home," Mike said. He saw disappointment cross José's face and he felt a twinge of guilt.

As he began to walk away, Dean ran over to him. "Give him a chance, Mike," he said in a low voice. "This game is all new to him."

"No," said Mike. "It's a waste of time. He'll

never learn. We spend half our time chasing the ball." He turned away from Dean abruptly and headed home.

He didn't want to lose José's friendship, but football was important to Mike. He looked forward to playing with his friends every night after school. But not any more! He wouldn't play as long as José played.

When he got home, there was still an hour until supper. Grandmother was sitting in the corner of the living room by the fireplace. "No football today?" she asked as Mike came in.

"Naw," Mike said. "They don't know how to play."

"Well, how about playing a game with me? My eyes are too tired to sew any more today."

Mike was about to say no, when a glint came into grandmother's blue eyes. She wagged her finger at him. "Come on now, I challenge you!"

Mike grinned. Why not? He had nothing better to do and he knew grandma would like it.

"All right," he said, "I'll go and pick one."

When Mike came back with the game, he set up a small table for them to play on. "Now here's how you play, grandma," Mike began. Then he outlined the rules to her. "Do you think you understand?"

Grandmother nodded. "I think so. But there's a lot to remember. You'll have to overlook it if

70

I make a few mistakes at first. I'll start." She spun the arrow that pointed to the numbers.

"No, no, grandma!" Mike interrupted. "We have to spin to see who starts. Whoever spins the highest number is the one who starts."

Mike spun a two and grandmother spun a five. "All right, now you start," Mike said. Grandmother began to move five spaces on the board.

"No, no, grandma!" Mike shouted again. "You have to spin again to see how many spaces to move. That first spin doesn't count in the game."

Grandmother ran her fingers through her gray hair. "Oh dear, I'm so sorry. It's such a long time since I played a game like this." She spun again—a four this time.

"Now what do I do?" she asked.

"Move your man four spaces," Mike replied. He was getting impatient. Surely grandmother remembered better than this.

They played for nearly half an hour, and grandmother kept making mistake after mistake. By the end of the game Mike felt annoyed. He didn't want to play another game. He had to keep telling grandmother what to do. She didn't know how to play at all.

He put the game away and went out into the back yard. He could hear the shouts from the football game. *I hope José doesn't play tomorrow night*, he thought.

But the next night as he walked home from school, he could see José with his thick black hair, standing in the midst of the usual gang. It looked as though Dean was trying to explain the game to José. *How could he be so patient?* Mike wondered.

He tried to slide past them without anyone noticing him, but José saw him.

"Hey Mike!" he called. "You goin' to play?" And he flashed a friendly grin.

"Naw," Mike said, "Got something else to do," he mumbled.

José's grin disappeared, and he looked puzzled.

"Never mind him," Mike heard Dean say, and the next minute José turned away.

Mike felt angry and guilty at the same time. *He couldn't play football, not the way José messed up the game. He couldn't!* He kicked at the rocks on the sidewalk. *Now he'd really lost José's friendship. Why couldn't he keep any friends?*

Just then Mitch Murphy came zooming by on his brand new two-wheeler. Mitch was several years younger than Mike and had received a new bike for his birthday.

"Hey you! Look where you're going!" Mike yelled after him. "Don't you know you're not supposed to ride your bike on the sidewalk?" Mitch skidded around in his driveway and

72

sped back to Mike. Then he screeched to a halt and stood feet astride the bicycle.

"What was that?" he said, grinning, showing the gap in his front teeth.

"You're not supposed to ride your bike on the sidewalk. It's against the law. Now get off it." Mike grabbed the handlebars and shook the bike.

Mitch's toothless grin vanished. "But mom says I can't ride my bike in the street. I'm not old enough."

"Then you'd better walk!" Mike growled, and he shook the bike again. "Go on! Walk!"

Mitch tugged at his bike. "Let go!" he yelled. Then Mike suddenly let go. Mitch yanked the bike at the same moment and landed in a jumbled heap on the ground. He began to cry.

"I hate you, Mike Davis. You're mean," he said as he untangled himself from the bike. "I used to be your friend, but I'm not any more. You'll *never* have any friends. You're too bossy —everybody says so." And with that he moved off, pushing his bike in the direction of home.

Mike stared after him. Was that true? *Did* everyone say he was too bossy? It was true he liked things to be done correctly—mom always teased him about that—but did that make him bossy?

Mike began to think over the last few days. No one else seemed to care that José couldn't play football the right way. Then there was that game with grandmother yesterday. He'd been annoyed because she didn't know the rules. Now he'd even tried to boss young Mitch around—and really, he admitted it was none of his business. Maybe he was too fussy, too impatient—too bossy.

Just then footsteps sounded behind him. "Hey Mike!" a voice called. It was José. "How'd you like to learn to play soccer?" he asked. "The others all agreed," he said, grinning and nodding in the direction of the football game. "I'm no good at football, but I know soccer. Come on," he begged, "I'll show you."

Mike hesitated, then he relaxed and grinned. "Okay," he said, "but I hope you'll be more patient with me than I was with you."

> Treat others as you want them to treat you.
>
> Luke 6:31 LB

Forgive me, Lord, when I'm impatient, and help me to be more loving, kind, forgiving. Thank you for being my friend always.

Disappointment Is Hard to Take

As his father came through the door, Rick knew he had some exciting news. Rick could always tell because of the funny lopsided grin he had.

"How was your day, Rick?" his father asked.

"Pretty good, I guess. Steve came over and helped me fix up the rigging on my model sail boat."

"That's good," said dad, grinning even more. "How'd you like to go for a sail in a *real* sail boat?"

Rick could hardly believe his ears, "A real sail boat? That would be fantastic! When? How? Whose?"

Mr. Howard laughed, "Now wait a minute. One question at a time. Do you remember Ken Larson who used to work for me a year or so ago—a tall, blond fellow? Used to coach the PeeWees?"

Rick nodded. He remembered Ken. Everybody called him "The Big Swede," because his family had come from Sweden years ago and Ken was so proud of it.

"Well," his father continued, "Ken and his dad bought a Venture 22 last year and they spend most Saturdays sailing. When I told him how crazy you were about sailing, he offered to take us out next Saturday. He said he'd give me a few lessons in sailing too."

"Wow, dad! Wait 'til I tell Steve! A Venture 22—that's great!" It wasn't the biggest sailboat in the world, but it was just the right size to really get the feel of sailing.

"We'll go to the harbor tomorrow and look it over," his father promised. "I'll pick you up after school."

At last 3:15 P.M. came, and there was dad in the parking lot, waiting for him. He flung his school books in the back seat and buckled up the seat belt. "Hoist the sail and cast off," he declared.

"Aye-aye, sir," dad replied with a laugh, as he eased the car out of the parking lot.

They had no trouble finding where the *Sea Snark* was berthed. She was a beauty—sleek and shiny. Her sails were neatly furled in a bright blue canvas cover that matched the trim of the boat. Rick put out a hand and touched her. She was real all right. The ropes on her mast flapped gently in the breeze making a pinging sound. In all his dreams, this was exactly the boat Rick would have liked to own.

They spent about half an hour inspecting the *Sea Snark*. They couldn't go aboard, because Ken wasn't there—but Saturday was only two days away.

Dad suggested they spend the rest of the afternoon looking around the harbor, and Rick agreed. There were many beautiful boats moored in the marina, but to Rick's way of thinking, none of them could match the *Sea Snark*. Oh, there were other Venture 22s, but to Rick, the *Sea Snark's* blue was just that much deeper, her rails gleamed brighter, and the way she sat in the water was perkier, than any other 22 there. Suddenly it seemed as if Saturday would never come.

But it did. The minute he was awake Rick leaped out of bed and pulled back the drapes. The sky was dull gray. Small puffs of clouds with flat bases, that looked like they had been sheared off, hung in layers against the bleak sky.

Not such a nice day, Rick thought, but he wouldn't let it dampen his spirits. He dressed swiftly and then pulled on an old red sweater that had belonged to his cousin. It was too big, but he would probably need something warm to wear if the sun didn't come out. He decided

to wear his tennis shoes so that he wouldn't mark the deck of the beautiful *Sea Snark.*

Downstairs, dad gazed out of the living room window. The lopsided grin was missing, and he was listening to the radio.

"What's up, dad?"

"The weather doesn't look too promising, son."

"Oh, it'll clear up," said Rick, "You know it's always cloudy first thing in the morning. It's early yet."

"I hope so, but the forecast isn't good," dad replied.

Rick refused to think about it. Of course it would clear up.

When they arrived at the *Sea Snark,* Ken was standing at the bow gazing out at the ocean. There were white caps on the waves and the sheared-off clouds scooted along, pushed by a stiff breeze. The ropes on the masts all around them were clanging instead of making the usual gentle *ping.*

"How does it look, Ken?" dad asked.

Ken turned to reply, a worried look on his face. "Not too good, I'm afraid. Think we'd better hang around for an hour or so and see whether it's going to get worse."

Rick's heart sank. Was it possible they wouldn't go?

Ken moved aft. He put his hand on Rick's head and ruffled his hair. "I'd hate to disappoint you, Rick, but the ocean's not something you fool around with in bad weather."

Rick nodded and tried to smile. A lump rose in his throat and he turned away and swallowed hard. He climbed aboard and began to inspect the rigging. But at the same time he was praying, "Dear God, please let us be able to go out today. *Please* let us. I want to go so badly." It was a selfish prayer he knew, but God must know how much he had been looking forward to this and it wasn't wrong to want to go.

Just then Ken spoke. "That settles it, I'm afraid. See the harbor patrol office over there? They just raised the red flag."

"What does that mean?" Rick asked.

"The triangular red flag is a small-craft warning. That means weather and ocean conditions are not suitable for small boats."

"Can't we go, then?" Rick asked, but he already knew the answer.

"I'm afraid not. I'm really sorry, but we can always go another day. I'm going to be away on a business trip for a month, starting Monday, but the first Saturday after I get back, we'll try again. How will that be?"

A whole month! That seemed like forever to Rick. But he nodded, not trusting himself to speak. In fact, he was afraid he was going to cry, so he jumped off the boat onto the dock and bent over the side, pretending to look for crabs.

He had never felt so disappointed. Why didn't God answer his prayer?

The next morning the sky had cleared, although it was still very windy. Why couldn't it have been like this yesterday, Rick thought as the family car swung into the church parking lot. Rick automatically glanced at the church notice board. He always liked to read the quotation that was put there each week. Some of them were intriguing, like the one a few weeks ago: "What's missing from CH—CH? U R"

Rick stretched his neck to read, as they passed by. "Our disappointments are God's appointments," he read. What did that mean, he wondered. He repeated the words over in his mind. *Could it mean that there is often a reason why things don't work out the way we plan them*, he wondered. *What reason would God have had for not allowing them to go sailing yesterday?*

By the time they got into church, the congregation was just beginning to sing the first hymn. Rick always tried to take part in everything, but it was hard to stop his mind from wandering. He had that problem every Sunday. When the choir sang, it was easier for Rick to listen because he knew the song. But after that came the announcements, and Rick was just about to tune out again.

Then he heard Pastor Leyland say, "We have a special request for prayer this morning. Ken

Larson was rushed to the hospital yesterday afternoon with appendicitis."

Rick was so stunned he didn't hear the rest of the announcement. The words buzzed in his head. "Will he be okay, dad?" he whispered.

"Take a week or two to get over it, as long as there aren't any complications," dad whispered. "Good thing we weren't out in that storm with him. You and I don't know much about sailing, and we'd really have been in trouble."

Immediately the quotation on the notice board flashed through Rick's mind. "Our disappointments are God's appointments." So *that* was God's reason. Rick thought of the tossing ocean and the small sailboat. He remembered Ken's words, "The ocean's not something you fool around with in bad weather."

A feeling of relief swept over him. He was glad they hadn't gone sailing after all.

> And we know that all that happens to us is working for our good if we love God and are fitting into his plans.

Rom. 8:28 LB

O Lord, when things don't go according to my plans, help me to believe that you know what is best, because you know the beginning and the ending. Help me to be satisfied even though I'm disappointed.

82

I Wish I Weren't So Shy

It was a busy Saturday morning on Fifth Street, and from his vantage point across the street, Craig had a good view of his dad's gas station. He decided to stay on this side of the street until he could locate exactly where dad was. Then he'd take his lunch to him as mom had asked and leave again before anyone saw him. Not that he'd done anything to be ashamed of, but he hated the good-natured teasing of the men who worked for his father. Dad said they were just being friendly, but Craig didn't know how to answer them.

He stood at the edge of the sidewalk and watched. Ken and Cal were working on a blue Chevrolet in the pits and Dan was hopping between the pumps, the phone, and a station wagon. There was no sign of dad.

Looks like they're short-handed again, Craig thought as Dan made another trip to the pumps. Only last week dad asked him if he would like to help out Saturdays at the station, but the thought of meeting all those people made Craig say no—even though he could have used the money.

As he watched, a beautiful yellow Porsche drove up to the pumps, a tall, dark-haired young man jumped out. Craig recognized him immediately. He was their new neighbor from down the street. Craig stared in envy. One day he'd own a car like that. He wished he had the courage to go over and get a closer look, but if he did, Ken would be sure to make a joke about the "boss's son," and Craig would flush with embarrassment. Or Dan would want to know how he was getting on in school and he'd stammer and stutter in reply. So he stayed where he was.

Eventually the yellow Porsche drove off and still there was no sign of dad. Where could he be? Craig began to feel jittery. Suppose he had to go over there and look for him?

Suddenly a hand came down on his shoulder. Craig jumped. He whirled around.

"Oh, hi, dad." Craig smiled in relief and handed him his lunch. "Where've you been?"

"Down at the Willow Plate having a cup of coffee," his father explained. If he wondered why Craig was lurking across the street instead of leaving the lunch in his office, he didn't say anything. Craig was thankful for that!

After lunch Craig decided to bike down to Brad's house. Brad was his best friend and they spent most of their free time together. Brad's easy manner and relaxed ways appealed to Craig. He wished some of it would rub off on him.

He was just about to leave for Brad's house when he noticed the yellow Porsche was parked down the street again. The tall dark-haired young man was there with a cloth in his hand, buffing the door panels. He must have just finished polishing the car because the yellow body work gleamed against the black trim and the chrome dazzled in the afternoon sun.

Just then Brad appeared at the corner farther down the street. He strolled up to the young man and fell into easy conversation. Craig watched. How he would love to go and talk too. But he hesitated. He didn't have Brad's easy way of making conversation. All he would do is stand around and stare at the car, groping for something to say. So he stayed on the driveway and watched from a distance. He hoped Brad would come down this way soon. But he didn't. He seemed deep in conversation. They were pointing at different features of the car. The owner went around to the front and opened up the hood. They looked in for a few

minutes and then moved around to the trunk. Next the owner opened the car door and Brad looked in.

Craig itched to get in on the conversation. He hovered in uncertainty, for several minutes. He was missing a perfect chance to get a close-up look at his favorite car. But every time he made a move to join them, a tense embarrassed feeling swamped him. Maybe he'd make a fool of himself by asking a dumb question. Or worse yet, maybe the owner would ask him a question he couldn't answer. He seemed paralyzed.

At last his curiosity got the better of him and he began to move in the direction of the Porsche.

Just as he moved down the street, the young owner strode around to the driver's seat and climbed in. Then Brad got in on the other side and the next moment they roared away.

Craig stood there with his mouth open. "Oh, no!" he thought. "If I'd only gone down there sooner! I could have had a ride too." He was furious with himself. How dumb could you get? He turned back to the house in deep disappointment.

Twenty minutes later Brad came knocking at the door. "Guess what!" he said, his face flushed with excitement.

"I know, I know," Craig said bitterly. "You had a ride in the Porsche."

"How did you know?" Brad asked in surprise. Craig told him, but he didn't say that he'd been too shy to go and join them.

Brad guessed anyway. "Gee, Craig," he said, "you should have joined us. You've got to *do* something about being so shy. You'll miss out on all the fun things."

Craig shrugged as though he didn't care. But he did. Deep inside he was irritated at himself and very disappointed.

Later, after Brad had gone home again, Brad's words rankled. *What did it take?* he wondered. *He couldn't go on like this all his life. Who knows what other good chances he'd miss. He'd missed the Porsche twice today.*

The picture of Dan at the station, filling the Porsche with gas and checking the oil this morning, flashed into his mind. Lucky Dan! he thought. The next best thing to owning a Porsche would be working on one. Then he had an idea. But almost as soon as it came to him, he rejected it. He couldn't do it. Then he shook himself angrily. *Here's another opportunity and I'm going to miss it. What's the matter with me?*

For a while Craig wrestled with himself. Part of him wanted to do it, but another side of him battled against it.

Just then the front door slammed and Craig heard his father in the hall. Taking a deep breath Craig made his decision.

With a determined step he went to meet his father.

"Hi, dad," he said. "Is that offer you made still good—I mean about working on the pumps on Saturdays?"

"It certainly is," dad replied. "We've been rushed off our feet down there today."

"Okay." Craig said. "It's a deal, I'll start next Saturday."

Dad looked surprised. "What made you change your mind?"

"Well, I figured I'd learn something about cars while I'm down there, and if I start putting my pay away now I'll have a good bit saved for my Porsche by the time I'm old enough to drive."

Inside, Craig was also thinking, "Maybe if I make myself meet new people I'll get over being shy and I won't miss any more opportunities like I did today."

If God is on our side, who can ever be against us?

Rom. 8:31 LB

O Lord, when I am shy, give me the confidence that comes from knowing that you love me just the way I am.

I Feel Like Giving Up

It was bad enough being left until last when they chose sides for a game of soccer. Red was used to that. But when he kept missing the ball, and someone called, "Red, Red, Should've-stayed-in-bed," Red was furious.

Why couldn't he kick the ball properly? He was sure he could kick it farther than anyone else in the class—if only he could get the timing right. But it was always the same. Just as the ball came towards him, it seemed to stop, and the next second it was too late.

He sat at the edge of the field and picked at the grass. Tomorrow he would tell Mrs. Meyers. He wouldn't go back for any more therapy. It wasn't helping at all. He was no better at kicking or catching than he was three months ago. His math was just as bad. He still reversed the numbers in his answers. Why, only this morning he told the math teacher six 9s are 45, when he really meant to say 54. As for spelling—well his English teacher was ready to quit.

He gave up two afternoons a week for therapy. *Two whole* afternoons of his own time. It wasn't worth it! He was just dumb and that's all there was to it.

He felt a twinge of guilt because he knew Mrs. Meyers didn't like him to think of himself as dumb. But what other word was there for it when his writing looked like he did it during an earthquake and he couldn't spell the same word right two days running?

But there *was* another word for it—a long word—and Red could hardly pronounce it, let alone spell it—*dyslexia.* But who'd ever heard of dyslexia? None of Red's friends had.

Red didn't know what it was or what caused it, but he knew that it made him get his letters and numbers in the wrong order. Even though he might have the right letters all set in his mind's eye, when he went to put it down on paper it came out wrong.

Worse yet—it meant that he could neither kick a ball nor catch one properly. And he got mixed up with left and right, early and late, before and after, and—and—Red snatched up a handful of grass. Oh, what was the use!

Then he remembered Mrs. Meyers' words:

"You don't really cure dyslexia. You learn to overcome it with patience and determination."

Well, I don't have much of either, he decided angrily.

School over at last, Red decided to bury himself in the TV cartoons so he could forget his problems for awhile. But his mother met him at the door.

"Do you remember the Trawicks who used to live next door?" she asked, holding a letter in her hand.

"Sure I remember them," Red replied. "I used to play with Julia. She's a year older than I am, isn't she?"

"That's right," mother said, and her face grew serious. "Julia was in a car accident nearly a year ago. She's confined to a wheelchair now, I think, from what her mother says."

Red was shocked. He could remember Julia challenged him to bicycle races. The older boys always wanted her to play baseball with them. She could hit as far as any of them, and run a lot faster. He couldn't imagine her stuck in a wheelchair.

"They're coming back to town for a week," mother continued, and want to drop by to see us on Tuesday. I guess you could miss your therapy class for once. I'm sure Julia would like to see you again."

Red nodded. He didn't tell his mother he'd been planning to miss the class anyway.

By Tuesday, Red hadn't changed his mind. Now all he had to do was convince his mother. He would start on that, he decided, as soon as the Trawicks left.

In spite of the wheelchair, Julia hadn't changed a bit. She looked a little paler than Red remembered, but when she began to tease him for his thick red hair, Red knew she was still the same old Julia. In fact, the wheelchair hardly seemed to slow her down. She even let Red push her around the old neighborhood. She didn't seem at all embarrassed by her wheelchair.

They had been outside for a couple of hours when Julia decided it was time to go in. Red figured she must be tired and followed her into the house.

"Hey, Mom," she called, wheeling into the living room. "It's time for my exercises."

"Why don't you let them go for today," Mrs. Trawick suggested. "You and Red could find something to do till supper time."

Julia's lips met in a thin line. "No, mother," she said firmly. "Nothing's going to make me miss my exercise. Dr. Grey said there's a chance I'll walk again if I keep it up. Well, I'm going to keep it up," she said, emphasizing every word. "I *will* walk again. You'll see!"

"If determination has anything to do with it, you certainly will," her mother replied.

Gently Mrs. Trawick lifted Julia out of the

wheelchair and helped her stand up. Julia placed her arm around her mother's neck. Gathering her long pink skirt, she began to take a step. Slowly, painfully, she made three or four steps. Then she asked Red for the wheelchair and sank down into it.

"I do this every day for 20 minutes or more, if I can," she explained, breathing deeply from the exertion.

"That's hard work!" Red exclaimed admiringly.

Julia grinned. "It's nothing to what I do every morning with the physiotherapist. Now *that's* hard work, and it hurts, too." She made a face. "Here, how about you getting on the other side of me. With two of you to help, I should make great progress."

Red took his place at her side and for 20 minutes Julia practiced walking. Her face became paler as the minutes went by, and the wispy curls were damp across her forehead. But she wouldn't give up.

At last Mrs. Trawick insisted that she had done enough. "Okay," Julia agreed, "but the next time we come to see Red, I'll be walking again."

Red was sure she would. He didn't think Julia would *ever* give up until she was walking. He felt a stab of guilt, looking at her now sinking deep into the wheelchair. Dark shadows of exhaustion showed on her face. Suppose she knew I wanted to give up my therapy, he thought. "Quitter!" She would say. The guilty feeling grew and stayed with him for the rest of Julia's visit.

All the same, Red was sorry to see her go. Julia waved and called through the car window, "See you next year."

Red nodded. He turned to go back into the house. If he really was going to quit his therapy class, he had to convince mom now. Tomorrow would be too late. His class was right after school.

"Mom, have you got a minute?" he began as they walked into the living room. But then he stopped. He remembered Julia struggling to take those few steps across the rug. How could he quit his therapy knowing what it was costing Julia to learn to walk?

Mom was waiting for him to continue. "What is it, Red?" she asked.

"Oh . . ." he hesitated. "Will you be sure to let Mrs. Meyers know I'll be there tomorrow? I don't want to miss both sessions this week."

Whatever you do, do well.

Eccles. 9:10 LB

O Lord, when I am tempted to give up, give me the extra strength to continue even when the going gets rough. Please take away my discouragement and fill me with hope.

The Day Almost
Everything Went Wrong

"Doug! Doug! Wake up! It's late. If you don't get up now, you'll be late for school."

Doug rolled over and groaned, "Oh, mother" he said, "Didn't the alarm go off *again?*" That was the second time this week.

"We'll have to get it fixed," his mother said. "But don't worry about that now. I'll wake Sharon and have breakfast ready in ten minutes."

Doug swung himself out of bed and dressed quickly. Then after gulping down his breakfast, he dashed to the bathroom to brush his teeth. But Sharon had beat him to it.

"Come on, Sharon," he hammered on the door. "You know we're late. Don't stand there looking at yourself in the mirror."

"Okay, okay. Just a minute!" At last Sharon

opened the door, hair brush in hand and her long blonde hair falling over her shoulders. Doug pushed past her and grabbed his toothbrush.

In a few minutes he was ready. If he ran he might just make the bus. He kissed his mother, grabbing her by the neck, scooped up his school books and raced out of the door.

The school bus was already coming down the hill. He kept running. The bus roared past him in a cloud of dust up to the bus stop where a group of students were standing.

Doug had almost reached the bus as the last student climbed aboard. He heard the doors close and his heart sank. But the other children had seen him and the doors opened again.

Doug staggered aboard and the driver glared at him. "That's the second time this week I've had to wait for you," he growled.

Doug flushed. "Sorry," he managed to say.

He sank down in the nearest empty seat. Thankfully he had 20 minutes now to catch his breath and gather his thoughts for the day. It was Friday; that meant a math test. Mrs. Hartman had said so yesterday. Doug wasn't ready for it either. He knew he shouldn't have watched that TV program last night, but it was so good, he couldn't bear to miss it. Well, maybe he could make up for a little lost time now. He still had a few minutes to look through his math book.

His math book! Where was it? Doug went through the books on his knee in disbelief. He was sure he'd brought it home. Then he remembered. He'd taken it upstairs to bed with him, thinking that if he woke early enough he could study before getting up.

Doug stared miserably out of the window. What a day this was going to be!

The math test was awful. Doug knew he'd done poorly and he'd only himself to blame. He shrank down in his seat as the papers were collected, vowing never to neglect studying for a test again.

But the worst wasn't over yet, for Mrs. Hartman had other work for the class to do, and Doug didn't have his text book. It was no surprise when Mrs. Hartman said he would have to make up the work at home.

By lunch time, however, Doug was feeling much happier, as he lined up in the cafeteria. "Lasagna for lunch" was the word passed down the line. *Things were turning out better*, thought Doug. Lasagna was his favorite school lunch.

When his turn came he picked up his tray and moved along the line as the kitchen helpers placed food on it. Wow! He was lucky. He got a large helping. Mmm! It all smelled so good he could hardly wait to devour it. He swung around from the line to go to his seat.

Too late, he saw Mrs. Hartman striding towards him.

Crash! Food, dishes, and tray went flying. Doug's plate of delicious lasagna landed upside down on Mrs. Hartman's foot!

Doug froze. The noisy clatter and chatter in the cafeteria stopped, and it seemed to Doug that every eye in the room was on him.

Then the air was filled with comments around him.

"Look out clumsy!"

"What a mess!"

"Boy are *you* in trouble!" Some of the students behind him in the line giggled.

Doug tried to apologize. He felt his face flush scarlet. Even the fact that Mrs. Hartman didn't blame him entirely—she had been in a hurry, she said—didn't make him feel much better. Somehow, between them they cleaned up the mess.

At last Doug sat down with another tray of food, listening to the ribbing from his classmates.

"Just because you got into trouble for not having your math book, doesn't mean you have to throw your dinner at her," snickered Bill Thurston.

Doug growled, "Shut up" and ate his lunch. But he had lost his appetite.

The rest of the afternoon passed uneventfully, and Doug breathed a sigh of relief as the end-of-school bell rang. As soon as he got home, he dumped his books on the kitchen table. Thank goodness it was Friday!

He could hear his sister in the living room. "Mom will be home in an hour," she called. "She's gone to the store."

Doug grunted in reply. Sharon was watching the TV as usual. She always got home before him and hogged the TV. *I never get to watch my favorite programs*, he thought.

He went out into the back yard. The hot wind stirred the thick-leaved maple tree. Doug went over to it and sat down in its shade, propping himself against the firm trunk.

What a day this had been! Why did everything go wrong for him? *Seems like I'm no good at anything*, he thought. *I'm clumsy, forgetful, and always in trouble. I'm no use to anyone.*

He hunched up his knees and glared into space.

"Hey, Doug!" It was Joey Shepherd from across the street, appearing around the corner of the house. His large brown eyes peered out from under a green cap. Joey was only a second grader, but Doug talked to him once in a while because he felt sorry for him. All the other kids on the block were several years older than Joey, and they never had time for him.

"The chain came off my bike. Could you help me fix it?"

Doug stirred reluctantly, but replied, "Sure. Bring it over. I'll do it."

"It's here in the driveway. I brought it over already because I *knew* you'd fix it. I asked Jack and Rick and Dave too. But they never do anything for me."

It took Doug only a few minutes to fix the bike. Joey was overjoyed. "Gee thanks, Doug! You're the best friend I have!"

"Glad to do it," Doug grinned and pulled the peak of Joey's cap down over his eyes.

Doug thrust his hands into his pockets and sauntered around into the back yard again. Well, maybe he was good for something after all.

Then he noticed the brown marks on the lawn. It was burning up under the hot dry wind and sun of the last few days. He unwound the hose and set up the sprinkler. It felt good to be doing something useful. He turned the water on and set the timer for thirty minutes. In thirty minutes this stretch of the back lawn would be nicely soaked. Then he'd have to move the sprinkler to another stretch.

Just then Doug heard the family car pull into the driveway.

"Oh Doug!" mom exclaimed as she came into the back yard. "I'm so glad you're home. I have a large sack of salt for the water softener in the trunk, and I can't lift it by myself. Could you help me?"

"Sure, mom," Doug said.

It *was* a large sack and heavy too, but Doug figured he could manage it.

"It's okay, mom," he said, "You don't have to help." He heaved the heavy sack upright. Then grasping it firmly around the middle he lifted it into the garage.

"Thanks, Doug," mother said with a sigh of relief. "I don't know what I'd do without you."

Doug brushed himself off. The praise felt good after such a bad day. Mom hadn't noticed the sprinklers yet. He knew she'd be pleased about that too. This was turning out to be a better day after all.

Just then mom paused as she was about to enter the house. She looked back at Doug. "You'll be happy to know I bought a new alarm clock while I was out," she said with a smile.

Doug grinned. Things were *definitely* improving.

> So don't be anxious about tomorrow. God will take care of your tomorrow too. Live one day at a time.
>
> Matt. 6:34 LB

Lord, when everything goes wrong, help me not to give up. Give me strength to keep going. Thank you for each new day when I can make a new start.

Some People Are Different

Jon balanced his stamp collection precariously on his knee. He was trying to do two things at once. He needed to stick in these last few stamps, but he also wanted to watch the Harlem Globetrotters on the TV. He placed the stamps carefully on the arm of the sofa and leafed through the album to the correct page, occasionally glancing at the TV.

Suddenly Timothy and his friend Nick came racing into the room.

"No rough housing," John yelled, shielding his stamp collection with his arm.

"C'mon, Tim," Nick giggled, ignoring Jon. "Give me a ride, give me a ride!" and he grabbed at Timothy's shirt. Tim whirled around and grabbed Nick, wrestling him to the floor.

"Look out!" Jon yelled again, but too late. Tim's arm swung out, caught the corner of Jon's stamp album, and knocked it flying.

"You M.R.," Jon bellowed. "Get out of here!"

The two younger boys stopped wrestling. "You're an M.R. yourself," Tim said, making a face at him.

Mother appeared in the doorway. "Tim and Nick, you play outside if you want to wrestle or Nick will have to go home" she said. "But first help Jon pick up his stamps."

At last calm was restored, and the two younger boys went outside. "What's an M.R.?" Mother asked, after they had gone.

"Mentally retarded," Jon growled. "And that's what those two are!"

Mother looked serious. "Do you know what *mentally retarded* means?"

"Sure I do. All the kids at school say it. We have a new class for M.R. kids. They're dumb —stupid—can't learn. They look weird, too."

"Do you know you have a cousin who is, as you call it, an M.R.?"

"I do?"

"Yes. Her name is Misty, Uncle Pat and Aunt Eleanor's little girl. And we just received a letter saying they're coming to stay with us a few days."

"They are?" said Jon in surprise. "Gee, Mom! Do they have to bring Misty? I mean—what will the kids say? They'll make fun of her—

and me." That wasn't really the reason Jon didn't want Misty to come, but he couldn't tell his mother that he didn't like retarded children because they looked weird. In fact, he was a little scared of them. He didn't know how to behave with them.

"Perhaps you can help your friends to understand retarded children. Then maybe they won't make fun of her. Misty is only five, and it's not her fault she's not like the other children. She's really very lovable," mother sighed.

Jon wasn't convinced. He had been looking forward to the week's vacation, but now he wasn't so sure. Having Misty here would spoil things for sure.

The day they arrived, Jon stayed in his room as long as he could, but eventually he had to go downstairs and meet his uncle and aunt and cousin Misty.

Uncle Pat and Aunt Eleanor hugged Jon, exclaiming over how he had grown and how handsome he was. But Misty had her back to him. She was petting Casey, the family cat, and making crooning noises to him.

Aunt Eleanor went over to Misty and said, "Misty, look who's here." She took Misty's arm and helped her stand up. "This is Jon," Aunt Eleanor said as Misty stood up and looked at Jon. Jon was surprised. She didn't look as weird as he'd expected. Oh yes, she had the flat face of other children like this. Mongoloid, mother had called them. And she had the almond-shaped eyes and pudge nose too. But the way Aunt Eleanor had her dressed made her look rather cute.

"Hi Misty," Jon said, wondering what else to say.

"Say 'Hi Jon,' " Aunt Eleanor said to Misty.

"Hi, Thon," Misty said.

"Ca-Ca," she said and pointed to the cat. "Ca-Ca" she said again in a harsh voice. Then she turned back to Casey and began to stroke his thick, soft gray fur. Casey didn't seem to mind, because he stretched out full length, his eyes closed. Jon could hear his loud purr.

"Misty loves animals," Aunt Eleanor said. "They seem to sense that she isn't going to hurt them."

Jon watched the little girl rub the cat's fur, making noises to it. He was surprised. He had expected to feel more embarrassed than this.

At the supper table it was difficult not to stare at Misty. Jon wished Timothy wouldn't stare too. Many times Aunt Eleanor had to say to her, "Use your spoon, Misty. This is your spoon." Jon was surprised at her patience, because Misty kept forgetting and wanting to use her fingers. When she used her spoon, often she missed her mouth and bits of food would drop on her lap or on the table. But Aunt Eleanor never got angry. She just kept on reminding Misty to use her spoon.

After supper, while Mom and Aunt Eleanor did the dishes, Uncle Pat looked at books with Misty. The little girl sat cuddled in his lap. They didn't read the pages but just looked at the pictures. Often Misty would try to say the words for what was in the pictures. She'd point clumsily to the book and then giggle noisily. Every few minutes she would throw her arms around Uncle Pat and squeeze him. Then she'd trace his sideburns or ear with her fat stubby fingers. Uncle Pat didn't seem to mind this treatment. In fact, he seemed to enjoy it.

It was clear to Jon that Uncle Pat and Aunt Eleanor really loved Misty. At first, that seemed strange, but then as Jon thought about it, it wasn't hard to see why. She was their little girl, and they loved her.

As the days passed, Jon didn't feel so awkward with Misty. He was beginning to understand her. He even took her outside one day and played ball with her for a while—but in the back yard. She wasn't very good at it anyway, but she seemed to enjoy herself.

That night, after supper, Misty came to Jon carrying a book. "Yeed, yeed," she said, tugging at his sleeve. Jon knew she wanted him to read to her.

He moved to one side in the oversized arm chair and Misty climbed up beside him. She smelled of perfumed talcum powder, because she had just gotten out of the bath. Jon had to admit she looked quite cute in her long green and gold housecoat, and shining hair. *If only she looked normal,* he thought sadly.

He took the book from her gently and began to point out the pictures as he'd seen Uncle Pat do. Misty sat quietly most of the time. She seemed sleepy.

Page by page Jon pointed to the pictures and talked slowly and clearly, repeating himself often. That helped her to learn, Uncle Pat had said. As he talked, Jon became aware of the deep rhythmic breathing of the little girl beside him. He looked at her pink face. She had fallen asleep.

Uncle Pat came into the living room. "You've made a friend, Jon" he whispered. "She doesn't let everyone read to her." Then he lifted Misty up out of the chair and carried her softly upstairs to bed.

The next day Misty and her parents were to leave. Jon went out into the circle to kick a ball around. It was safe out there. Only a few cars ever came into the circle. He needed to keep out of the way of the confusion of all the packing and carrying of suitcases. Timothy had gone over to Nick's house.

Just then Aunt Eleanor came to the door, with Misty at her elbow.

"Would you please watch Misty for us, Jon? We're almost done. Just a few more things and we'll be ready to go."

"Sure," said Jon without a second thought. "Come on, Misty, I'll show you how to kick a ball."

Misty ran out, her heavy shoes clomping. She had trouble kicking the ball, but judging by her squeals and giggles she seemed to be having a good time.

"No, no, Misty. Look, like this." Jon demonstrated, kicking the ball gently towards her.

At that moment Ted O'Hara rode up on his bike. He watched them for a few minutes, then he said, "Who's the kid?"

"Oh that's Misty. She's my cousin," Jon replied. Then he realized why Ted was staring. He was surprised at himself. After only a few days, Jon had almost forgotten that Misty was retarded. He picked up the ball.

"Come here, Misty," he said and he took her hand. "This is Ted. Say 'Hi Ted.'"

"Hi Thed," Misty said in her funny way.

"It's okay," Jon said to Ted, when he saw him looking uncomfortable. "She's a good kid," he said. He searched for words to put him at ease. "She's really not much different from you and me and she needs friends, too."

God has given each of us the ability to do certain things well.

Rom. 12:6 LB

Forgive me, Lord, when I forget that you love and care for everybody no matter how different they are from me. Help me to remember that everyone is special to you.